YOU ARE THE STAR
～ of a ～
Muppet Adventure

Featuring Jim Henson's Muppets™

YOU ARE THE STAR
～ of a ～
Muppet Adventure

Featuring Jim Henson's Muppets™

By Ellen Weiss
Illustrated by Benjamin Alexander

Muppet Press/Random House

Library of Congress Cataloging in Publication Data:
Weiss, Ellen.
You are the star of a Muppet adventure.
SUMMARY: Kermit and the rest of the Muppets try to catch their runaway chickens. The reader participates in the story and controls the action by selecting specific pages to turn to.
[1. Puppets—Fiction. 2. Literary recreations] I. Henson, Jim. II. Alexander, Benjamin, ill. III. Title. PZ7.W4472Yo 1983 [E] 83-4028 ISBN: 0–394–85623–6
Manufactured in the United States of America   1 2 3 4 5 6 7 8 9 0

For Mel and Nora
—E.W.

☆ ☆

Don't turn the page until you read this!

This is a very special Muppet book. Because you don't just read it, you're IN it—right next to Kermit, Miss Piggy, and their Muppet friends. And what happens in the book depends on you!

Here's how it works. Start reading on page 3, and keep on reading until you have to make a choice. Do you want to be silly or sensible? Brave or cautious? When you make up your mind, turn to the page for that choice and see what happens!

When you finish one story, go back and start again. There are all kinds of Muppet adventures in this book, and *you* are the star of each one.

Are you ready for some Muppet mayhem? Then turn to page 3—and have fun!

One Saturday you're sitting in front of your house, fixing the brakes on your bike. Suddenly a wild-eyed group of chickens goes tearing by.

"Camilla! Come back! I can't live without you!" cries a familiar voice. Looking down the street, you see a strange figure streaking along after the chickens.

"It's Gonzo!" you think in amazement. "What's he doing on my street?" But your thoughts are interrupted by the sight of a puffing, panting herd of Muppets running after Gonzo.

Bringing up the rear is . . . yes, it's really Kermit the Frog himself, still trying to button his shirt.

"Don't run away, Camilla!" puffs Kermit. "You heard the Swedish Chef all wrong! He was saying he had to *check* in the pot, not put a chicken in the pot!"

☆ ☆ ☆ ☆ ☆ ☆ ☆ ☆ ☆ ☆ ☆ ☆ ☆ ☆ ☆ ☆ ☆ ☆ ☆ ☆

Turn the page.

But Camilla and her friends don't seem to hear Kermit. They are running faster and faster, in a panic at the thought of being Swedish chicken soup. In their fright they don't even notice that they're heading straight for the railroad tracks.

As Kermit runs past, he sees you and your bike. "Wheels!" he says. "Just what we need! Can you help us catch our chickens? We're desperate!"

You're a little uncertain. It will only take you another minute to fix your brakes. Then your bike will really be safe to ride. Suddenly you hear a train whistle in the distance.

☆ ☆

If you decide to finish fixing your brakes first, turn to page 6.

If you decide to jump on your bike and hope for the best, turn to page 8.

"Just one more bolt," you say to yourself, "and the brakes will work."

But before you can finish, Gonzo comes whizzing up to you. "Wowee!" he exclaims, "a bicycle! Ah-ha, I can see that the problem is your back wheel. It needs to have a little more shimmy. Here, let me have a look. I once fixed a whole bicycle with a tongue depressor."

He climbs onto the bike, sitting backward on the seat. The bike begins to move, but Gonzo doesn't notice.

"Gonzo, be careful," you warn. "It's not the back wheel that's broken, it's the—" But it's too late. The bike is heading down the hill, straight for the river.

"—brakes!" you finish.

"Wow!" Gonzo says. "What a trip!"

The only good part is that the chickens have stopped running to watch their beloved Gonzo.

The way you figure it, you might be able to jump onto the bike with Gonzo and stop it somehow. Or you could run after Gonzo and try to save him when he lands in the river.

☆ ☆

If you decide to jump onto the bike with him, turn to page 21.

If you decide to fish Gonzo out of the river, turn to page 22.

You jump on your bike, pedaling after the chickens. Kermit hops onto the handlebars.

"Gee, thanks," he pants. "How do you do? I'm Kermit the Frog."

"I'm _____ the Kid," you (your name) reply. "Pleased to meet you."

You pick up speed, and soon you can hear the clatter of the freight train. It's traveling fast. So are the chickens.

"I don't know if Camilla can take all this excitement," worries Kermit.

"She's no spring chicken," agrees Miss Piggy, running alongside you.

"Hey, watch that fowl language," says Fozzie Bear. "Gonzo loves those chickens."

"I've got to stop that train somehow," you declare.

"Or you've got to stop the chickens," Kermit adds.

☆ ☆

If you decide to try to stop the train,
turn to page 10.

If you decide to try to stop the chickens,
turn to page 12.

"Okay, I'm going to stop that train!" you say bravely. You jump off your bike and stand near the tracks, wondering how you're going to do it. It's thundering closer every second.

"I have an idea," says Fozzie Bear, taking off the red handkerchief he wears around his neck. "Here—wave this at the train. Trains always stop when you wave a red bandanna at them."

You grab the bandanna and wave it at the locomotive.

It works! With a deafening screech of brakes, the train comes to a stop about two inches from Camilla's tail feathers.

"Yaaay!" yells everyone.

"Hey, look at this train," says Gonzo. He points to a large sign on the side of the first car:

COMMANDER CATNIP'S TRAVELING
USED BLIMP AUCTION

"Howdy, folks," calls a man with red suspenders and a silver beard. "Come on in and look around."

☆ ☆ ☆ ☆ ☆ ☆ ☆ ☆ ☆ ☆ ☆ ☆ ☆ ☆ ☆ ☆ ☆ ☆ ☆ ☆

Turn to page 14.

How on earth are you going to stop the chickens?

Suddenly you have an idea. You pedal as fast as you can, until you're just within earshot of the chickens. Then you start talking in a loud voice:

". . . So you see, sir, I've been sent all over the world to seek out the most talented, beautiful, intelligent, gifted chickens . . ." The chickens begin to slow down. ". . . to enter the Chicken of the Year Contest, which, as you know, brings fame and fortune to the lucky winner."

By the time you finish your sentence, the chickens have skidded to a halt. In a cloud of dust, they turn and stampede back in your direction, away from the train tracks.

"Where do we enter?" clucks Camilla breathlessly.

"Sorry, it was a lie," you say. "But it did save your lives."

And, indeed, at that moment the train is barreling through the crossing, right where the chickens would have been a second ago.

A big cheer goes up, and everyone claps you on the back.

"You've saved our chickens!" Kermit says. "How can we thank you?"

"Why don't you come back to the theater with us?" asks Fozzie.

"We could give you the grand tour," offers Miss Piggy.

"Or the Swedish Chef could cook you a wonderful dinner—er, a vegetarian one," says Scooter.

☆ ☆ ☆ ☆ ☆ ☆ ☆ ☆ ☆ ☆ ☆ ☆ ☆ ☆ ☆ ☆ ☆ ☆ ☆ ☆

*If you decide on the grand tour,
turn to page 18.*

*If you decide on the Swedish Chef's
dinner, turn to page 16.*

There's a used blimp auction going on when you get inside, and the auctioneer is talking very fast.

"We're offering this blimp at four hundred fifty-eight thousand dollars," he says. "At that price it's a steal. Do I hear four hundred fifty-nine thousand dollars?"

"Ugh, there's a fly on my nose," mutters Fozzie, swatting it away.

"SOLD! To the bear in the bow tie, for four hundred fifty-nine thousand dollars!" yells the auctioneer. "Shall I wrap it up, or do you want to fly it home?"

"Wait a second, wait a second!" says Fozzie. "Oh, sir, excuse me! I didn't want to buy that blimp. I don't have four hundred fifty-nine thousand dollars."

"Well, how much do you have?" asks the auctioneer.

Fozzie reaches into his pocket. "A nickel."

"SOLD!" yells the man. "To the bear in the bow tie, for one nickel!"

Fozzie is thrilled. "Oh, the bear is lucky," he says. "A real blimp! Maybe I'll go on a trip around the world. Do you want to come along?"

☆ ☆

If you decide to accept his invitation, turn to page 38.

If you decide not to go with him, turn to page 40.

"Dinner made by the Swedish Chef sounds like fun," you say. You go back to the theater and the Chef runs around, throwing things into pots and chopping up who-knows-what. At last he's made an amazing dinner. The trouble is, you can't understand a word he says when you ask what you're eating.

But you have lots of fun anyway. Dinner with the Muppets is not like dinner at home. Especially with Animal swinging from the chandelier and roaring, "MORE FOOD!"

As you finish, the Chef appears, wanting to know what you'd like for dessert. You have your choice of Flögenbörp or Dørbentøoten.

Hmmm . . .

☆ ☆ ☆ ☆ ☆ ☆ ☆ ☆ ☆ ☆ ☆ ☆ ☆ ☆ ☆ ☆ ☆ ☆ ☆ ☆

If you choose Flögenbörp,
turn to page 34.

If you choose Dørbentøoten,
turn to page 46.

"I'd love to come back to the theater with you," you say. "I've never been backstage before."

Animal hoists you onto his shoulders, and you all troop back to the theater in high spirits.

When you get there, you find a large sign on the stage door: CLOSED UNTIL FURTHER NOTICE.

"What now?" sighs Kermit. "Have they condemned the building?"

You hear a cackling sound coming from behind the door. Flinging it open, you find Statler and Waldorf, caught in mid-cackle.

"What's all this?" Kermit asks them.

"Well, you all rushed out, so we took the opportunity of closing this place down," says Statler. "Now we won't have to watch any more of your terrible shows for a while."

"And don't try to come in," warns Waldorf. "We've got the place booby-trapped."

"Impossible!" says Miss Piggy. "Let's just go in. Nothing will happen."

"But what if the place really is booby-trapped?" says Fozzie. "We'd better not go in."

☆ ☆ ☆ ☆ ☆ ☆ ☆ ☆ ☆ ☆ ☆ ☆ ☆ ☆ ☆ ☆ ☆ ☆ ☆

If you decide to go in, turn to page 29.

If you decide not to go in, turn to page 28.

You actually manage to jump onto the bike with Gonzo. You try dragging your feet to stop it, but you're going too fast. Gonzo isn't helping much: he's singing "Bicycle Built for Two" at the top of his lungs.

You try the hand brake, but it snaps off in your hand.

Down the hill you career, faster and faster, right off the end of the dock, and—

CRASH! You haven't hit the water at all. Instead, you've landed right on top of a passing barge. You dust yourselves off, look around, and see—*bowling balls*? Yes, that's what they are. Hundreds of bowling balls. The barge is piled high with them.

☆ ☆ ☆ ☆ ☆ ☆ ☆ ☆ ☆ ☆ ☆ ☆ ☆ ☆ ☆ ☆ ☆ ☆ ☆

Turn to page 24.

"Don't worry, Gonzo, I'll save you!" you shout, running down the hill as fast as you can. Gonzo and the bike land far out in the water with a loud splash.

Gonzo doesn't come to the surface. The water is very still. Has he drowned already? The chickens start to sob.

You take a flying leap into the water and start swimming for all you're worth. Can you find him and pull him out in time?

"Hi, everybody!" says a familiar, cracked voice. You look up and there's Gonzo, treading water. There's a fish in his ear.

"Gonzo!" you shout. "Thank goodness you're safe! What's that fish doing in your ear?"

"I can't hear you," says Gonzo. "There's a fish in my ear." He takes it out and throws it into the water. "I've just worked out a dynamite new act," he announces. "Get this: The Great Gonzo Rides a Bicycle Under Water While Whistling

a Tune with a Fish in One Ear! It'll be
the hit of the year!"

Camilla and her friends clap madly.
You can only shake your head in amazement.

You never do get your bike back, but
you do get free tickets to Gonzo's show.

END

You hear someone talking below deck: "Hey, Duke, what was that noise up there? I heard a crash."

"Nah, it was only a bowling ball falling. Keep reading what it says in the *Daily Doily*," says Duke.

"Okay, boss. Here it is: 'BIG BOWLING BALL HEIST. Early this morning five hundred sixty-eight specially autographed Bowling Balls of the Stars were stolen from the Bowling Hall of Fame. The thieves are still at large.' Haw, haw—and we're going to stay at large too," guffaws the first voice.

"Well, Gonzo," you whisper, "here we are with five hundred sixty-eight stolen bowling balls. What do we do now?"

"Let's just stay up here and see what happens. Kind of groove with it," suggests Gonzo.

Then you hear footsteps. "Maybe we should jump off," you say nervously.

☆ ☆

If you decide to stay on the barge, turn to page 26.

If you decide to jump, turn to page 36.

Duke and his friends come up on deck. They're playing a game of catch with the bowling balls when they notice you and Gonzo.

"What's this?" asks Duke.

"Never mind this—what's that?" says someone else, looking at the deck. There is water covering it. The barge is beginning to sink!

"Quick," orders Duke, "look in the barge instruction book."

Somebody comes up with the manual and begins to read:

" 'Caution! Do not overfill barge. Its capacity is five hundred sixty-eight bowling balls. Or four hundred bowling balls, one bicycle, one kid, and one weird character.' "

"How many bowling balls do we have?" asks Duke.

"Five hundred sixty-eight."

"So. We have to throw a bunch of bowling balls overboard, or we have to get rid of these two." There's a moment of silence. Then Duke and his friends start coming toward you.

Gonzo pokes you in the ribs. "We can talk our way out of this," he whispers. "Let me handle it."

Putting your fate in Gonzo's hands is a little scary. You might be better off letting the crooks throw you overboard.

☆ ☆

If you decide to let Gonzo try to get you out of it, turn to page 52.

If you decide to take your chances overboard, turn to page 48.

28

While you're all standing around outside the theater, you hear something strange approaching. It's making a loud, mechanical clucking noise.

Down the street comes the oddest thing you've ever seen. It's a large truck, covered with brown and white spots and flashing lights. On its roof is a giant chicken head that's revolving slowly. The loud clucking noises are coming from its beak.

☆ ☆ ☆ ☆ ☆ ☆ ☆ ☆ ☆ ☆ ☆ ☆ ☆ ☆ ☆ ☆ ☆ ☆ ☆ ☆

Turn to page 50.

"Of all the nerve!" huffs Miss Piggy. "Statler and Waldorf wouldn't know a true *artiste* if they tripped over one. I'm going in there."

She barges into the theater. "Excuse *moi*," she says, brushing past Statler. Statler bumps into Waldorf, and together they crash into the door. This sets off their booby trap, a pail of water that empties right onto their heads.

"Drat!" sputters Waldorf.

"Double drat!" sputters Statler.

"You're better off this way, you guys," says Kermit. "After all, what would you do without the show to complain about?"

Before they can answer, Scooter comes rushing over to Kermit. "Boss!" he says. "We've got a really big problem on our hands."

☆ ☆ ☆ ☆ ☆ ☆ ☆ ☆ ☆ ☆ ☆ ☆ ☆ ☆ ☆ ☆ ☆ ☆ ☆ ☆

Turn to page 32.

And so, ten minutes later, with a polka-dot costume and butterflies in your stomach, you're center stage with the spaghetti jugglers. Somebody flips you a mess of noodles.

"Hey, I'm getting the hang of it," you say in amazement. "This is fun!"

In fact, you turn out to be a truly inspired, great spaghetti juggler. You go on to become world famous, and this performance goes down in history as the night you got your start!

END

"What's the problem?" says Kermit.

"The show's about to start, and two of our acts are falling apart."

"Which ones?" asks Kermit with a sigh.

"Well, you remember those spaghetti jugglers you hired? The head juggler can't go on. He ate all the spaghetti last night and now he has a stomachache."

"Great," says Kermit, his head in his hands. "What's the other problem?"

"The monsters. They're on strike. They're supposed to do a big dance number, but they don't have a song. They want a special song, like Miss Piggy gets."

"One of these days I'm going to retire to a nice quiet swamp!" moans Kermit. "Where are we going to get a new spaghetti juggler and a new song? I can't spare anybody—everyone here has a part in the show."

Suddenly, in the silence that follows, everyone in the room turns to you.

"Want a little job?" asks Kermit.

Your new friends are in trouble, and you can't let them down. But song writing? *Spaghetti juggling?*

☆ ☆ ☆ ☆ ☆ ☆ ☆ ☆ ☆ ☆ ☆ ☆ ☆ ☆ ☆ ☆ ☆ ☆ ☆ ☆

If you decide to go on with the spaghetti jugglers, turn to page 30.

If you decide to try writing a song for the monsters, turn to page 37.

"I'll have the Flögenbörp," you say uncertainly.

"I think you pronounced that wro—" says Kermit, but not in time. There's a big puff of blue smoke, and out of it appears a large character in floppy pants.

"Hergen dørten oop genie!" says the Chef, jumping up and down.

Scooter flips through his Swedish Chef dictionary in a hurry. "It seems," he explains, "that when you pronounced that word wrong, what you *did* say was the magic word to summon this Swedish genie."

"Dorg pörp hand, oot brg wish," says the genie.

"He says he's got a wish in each hand, and you should pick one."

☆ ☆

If you choose the right hand,
turn to page 53.

If you choose the left hand,
turn to page 58.

You and Gonzo take a deep breath, count to three, and get ready to jump off. But wait! Should you jump to the left or to the right? Decisions, decisions!

☆ ☆

If you decide to jump to the left,
turn to page 42.

If you decide to jump to the right,
turn to page 44.

You write a nice little dancing song
for the monsters, and it goes like this:

It's time to put on earmuffs,
It's time to run and hide,
It's time to meet the monsters,
So you'd better stand aside.

It's time to find the exit
Or crawl beneath your seat;
We're gonna do the rhumba
With our size 100 feet!

END

You and Fozzie have a lovely time, floating peacefully over the world. Everywhere people wave and you wave back.

Then, somewhere over the sunny South Pacific, you hear a loud hissing noise.

Oh, no! Your blimp has sprung a leak!

"Maybe we can make it to that island," you say. And you do. You touch down gently on the pink sand of a beautiful tropical island. The natives all crowd around to greet you.

Wait a minute—something is strange about these natives. Why, each one is wearing a funny nose and glasses! And the one who looks like the chief is wearing a rubber chicken around his neck!

Fozzie is so excited he can hardly talk. "Do you know where we *are*?" he cries. "We're on the legendary Lost Island of Funnibonia, the place where all the jokes in the world come from! I always thought it was just a fairy tale!" He walks over to shake the chief's hand and slips on a banana peel. Everybody laughs, including Fozzie.

Needless to say, the bear is in heaven. The blimp is ruined and you're marooned, but Fozzie doesn't mind staying there. In fact, after a while, he's elected King of Funnibonia.

You, however, can't stand all the terrible jokes. You spend your time building rafts, balloons, and boats, fruitlessly trying to get back to civilization.

END

Fozzie decides he'll take his trip alone. He spends the next few hours blowing up his blimp, only to find that it has several big holes. It's useless.

The blimp is made of hundreds of yards of red-and-blue-striped material. "Hmmm," ponders Fozzie. "What can I do with all this blimp?

"I've got it!" he says at last. "Listen, in your opinion, how do most people feel about bears?"

"I guess they're scared of them," you say.

"But they aren't scared of me!" he says. "You know why? It's because I have a bow tie." His eyes are shining as he continues. "I have a dream. If I use all this material, I can make thousands—maybe millions!—of bow ties. Every bear in this country can have one. Then nobody will be scared of them anymore. It'll be wonderful!"

And so a company called Bow Ties for Bears, Inc., is formed, and Fozzie names

you Chairkid of the Board. Pretty soon
the woods are ringing with the sounds of
"Wocka-wocka!" and "Oh, the grizzly bear
is funnee!"

END

You jump to the left and land in the water, and something strange happens—you're pulled down, down to the bottom of the river. "Good-bye, Gonzo," you bubble. That's the last thing you remember before you wake up.

When you open your eyes, Gonzo is with you. You're still under water, but you can breathe, and you're at the center of an incredible shining city. A beautiful princess stands before you, smiling.

"Wh-where are we?" you ask.

"You have found the Lost Continent of Atlantis," she says.

☆ ☆

Turn to page 55.

You and Gonzo jump off to the right. The water is very cold. Luckily, you're a good swimmer—but it's a lot harder with Gonzo wrapped around your neck.

What's this? Way off yonder, you see Animal in the water, waving to you. You strike out toward him. He's so big and strong, he'll save you.

But wait—what's that? Way off in the opposite direction, you see Robin. He's waving to you, and he seems to be with

some friends. There are an awful lot of them. Maybe they'll save you. Which way should you head?

☆ ☆

If you decide to swim toward Robin, turn to page 49.

If you decide to swim toward Animal, turn to page 56.

After a while the Swedish Chef comes back carrying a huge covered platter. He removes the cover with a flourish, and you see a strange yellowish-green mound. It's quivering. You turn pale.

"What is this stuff?" you ask Scooter.

Scooter consults his Swedish Chef dictionary. "Let's see," he says. "Dørbentøoten—ah, here it is. It's listed as Twirling Turnip Surprise."

Suddenly the yellowish-green mound gets up and begins to tap and twirl across the platter. The Swedish Chef beams like a proud father.

"Does this mean I don't have to eat it?" you ask Scooter.

"I guess so," he answers.

"Thank goodness," you sigh.

When the turnips are finished, they take a deep bow. Then they tap off the table and out the door.

"Whew!" you think. "That was close!"

END

You're wondering how long you can tread water when you see a ship passing. You call out, and soon you and Gonzo are hauled aboard.

"How can we ever thank you?" you say.

"You can't," the captain answers.

"Where are you headed?" you ask.

"Down to the South Pole," he replies. "We're doing the penguin census. It will take us about a year to count all the penguins. Unless we lose count, that is. Then we have to start all over again."

"Well, that's interesting. If you could just drop us off at the next dock—"

"Sorry, we can't do that. We stopped once to pick you up, and now we're behind schedule. You'll have to come with us."

'Bye!

END

Good choice! Robin is out practicing with his Junior Frogman troop. All twelve of them swim over to save you. They float you easily to shore.

You unwrap Gonzo from around your neck and thank Robin and his friends.

"Don't mention it," says Robin. "We were hoping somebody would fall in the water. Now we can all get our Frog Scout lifesaving badges."

END

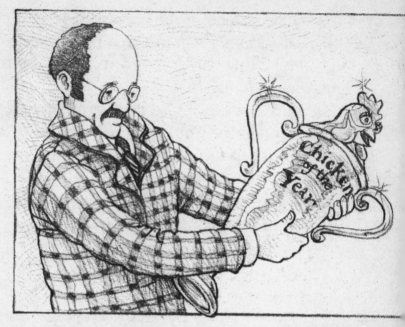

You're scared, but you're curious. You watch as the truck lurches to a stop. Will a Martian pop out?

No. It's just a man in a plaid suit. "Hiya," he says. "I represent the Chicken of the Year Contest, and I have an award here for Camilla the Chicken. Does she live here?"

"The what? You mean, there really *is* a Chicken of the Year award?"

"Why certainly," he says, looking insulted. "It's very famous."

With tears streaming down her beak, Camilla accepts her prize. "I'd like to thank my mother and father and, of course, Gonzo," she weeps.

"Well, I'll be," you whisper to yourself.

END

"Hey, listen, you guys," says Gonzo. "The way you handle those bowling balls— it's sensational! You fellas are natural showmen! We could use you in our show."

"For real?" asks Duke, turning red.

"Yeah, for real. Why don't you give up your life of crime and come be in show biz?"

After giving back the bowling balls and apologizing, the robbers join the show. Instead of using bowling balls, they decide to do a mind-reading act with fleas. And the whole world is shocked to find out what fleas really think about!

END

Well, it looks as if the right hand was a mistake. You've turned into a frog!

"Greep!" you croak.

Kermit comes rushing over to you. "Congratulations!" he says. "Welcome to the frog world! You're really going to like it. Let's see—first I'll take you down to the swamp for some singing practice. Then I'll introduce you to my cousin Al. He can get you a nice lily pad in a good neighborhood. Then we can go to the Frog Boutique, and . . ."

END

You and Gonzo spend three wonderful days and nights in Atlantis. The gentle people feed you and tell you magical stories. You're sad when you have to go.

"Where have you been?" ask your parents when you get home. "We've been frantic with worry!"

"On the Lost Continent of Atlantis!" you say. "It was really neat!"

Now your parents look *very* worried. They call the doctor.

"The child has had a terrible shock, but will be sane again soon," says the doctor.

The harder you try to convince people you were on Atlantis, the less they believe you. Naturally, nobody believes Gonzo, either. After a while you start to wonder whether it happened at all. Except when Gonzo winks at you.

END

You finally make it over to Animal. He's still waving his arms. "Here we are," you gasp. "You can save us now."

Animal keeps waving his arms. "GLUB," he says.

"He's not waving to us," Gonzo tells you. "He can't swim. We have to save *him*."

"What do you mean, *we*?" you gasp.

You sigh, take a deep breath, and tow Animal and Gonzo to shore.

"ANIMAL LOVES YOU!" he bellows when he can breathe again. He tries to give you a hug, but you duck. Poor Gonzo gets it instead.

Your parents are so glad to have you back that they ask Animal and Gonzo to stay for dinner. Animal eats all the doorknobs and Gonzo polishes off the toothpaste.

"Wow! Your dad's a great cook!" says Gonzo.

"MORE DOORKNOBS!" cries Animal.

Finally they leave. And from that day on, whenever you bring friends home for dinner, your parents hide the toothpaste!

END

58

You wish for all the Muppets to live happily ever after. And they do.

END